What the
BIBLE
Says
about
EMOTIONS

What the
BIBLE
Says
about
EMOTIONS

BARBOUR
PUBLISHING

© 2009 by Barbour Publishing

ISBN 978-1-60260-281-6

Scripture quotations marked NIV are taken from the HOLY BIBLE, NEW INTERNATIONAL VERSION®. NIV®. Copyright © 1973, 1978, 1984 by International Bible Society. Used by permission of Zondervan. All rights reserved.

Scripture quotations marked NASB are taken from the NEW AMERICAN STANDARD BIBLE®, copyright © 1960, 1962, 1963, 1968, 1971, 1972, 1973, 1975, 1977, 1995 by The Lockman Foundation. Used by permission.

Scripture quotations marked NCV are taken from the NEW CENTURY VERSION®. Copyright © 2005 by Thomas Nelson, Inc. Used by permission. All rights reserved.

Scripture quotations marked NLT are taken from the Holy Bible, New Living Translation, copyright © 1996, 2004. Used by permission of Tyndale House Publishers, Inc., Wheaton, Illinois 60189, U.S.A. All rights reserved.

Scripture quotations marked CEV are taken from the Contemporary English Version, copyright © 1991, 1992, 1995 by the American Bible Society. Used by permission.

Scripture quotations marked NKJV are taken from the New King James Version®. Copyright © 1982 by Thomas Nelson, Inc. Used by permission. All rights reserved.

Scripture quotations marked MSG are taken from THE MESSAGE. Copyright © by Eugene H. Peterson 1993, 1994, 1995, 1996, 2000, 2001, 2002. Used by permission of NavPress Publishing Group.

Scripture quotations marked ESV are taken from The Holy Bible: English Standard Version®, copyright © 2001 by Crossway Bibles, a publishing ministry of Good News Publishers. Used by permission. All rights reserved.

Published by Barbour Publishing, Inc., P.O. Box 719, Uhrichsville, Ohio 44683, www.barbourbooks.com

Our mission is to publish and distribute inspirational products offering exceptional value and biblical encouragement to the masses.

 Member of the
Evangelical Christian
Publishers Association

Printed in the United States of America

CONTENTS

INTRODUCTION

THE COLOR
OF LIFE

Emotions give color to living. Everyday events become lasting memories based on the feelings they evoke in our hearts. Activities in themselves are just busyness—but the thrill and the pain of life drive us either to praise or to cry out to God.

Through the highs and the lows—and the vast shades of emotion found in between— God draws us into a deeper appreciation of the life He's given us. Joys are sweeter when we have known pain; anguish hurts more if we have known true happiness. Taken together, this spectrum of emotion allows us to better understand ourselves, others, and God.

CHAPTER 1

EMOTIONS OF LOVE

My most precious memories and deepest joys revolve around the times when I've given or received love. Of course, that includes roman-tic love—but I'm also talking about the genuine affection and tender concern that I've known in many of my relationships. Each time I find myself in the middle of one of these love-filled moments, I feel so full of life—as though I'm experiencing the true reason for living. I feel so connected to God and to His love when I can see a glimpse of it reflected in His world. I'm amazed when I stop to think that God could have created us without emotions at all, yet He gave us something as pre-cious as the ability to love the way He's loved us.

■ Samantha, age 46, Alabama ■

AFFECTION

■ Don't just pretend to love others. Really love them. Hate what is wrong. Hold tightly to what is good. Love each other with genuine affection, and take delight in honoring each other.

ROMANS 12:9–10 NLT

■ Husbands, love your wives and do not be harsh with them.

COLOSSIANS 3:19 NIV

■ For I have derived much joy and comfort from your love, my brother, because the hearts of the saints have been refreshed through you.

PHILEMON 1:7 ESV

■ We loved you so much that we were delighted to share with you not only the gospel of God but our lives as well, because you had become so dear to us.

1 THESSALONIANS 2:8 NIV

CARING

■ Let's see how inventive we can be in encouraging love and helping out.

HEBREWS 10:24 MSG

■ Be devoted to one another in brotherly love. Honor one another above yourselves.

ROMANS 12:10 NIV

■ If anyone considers himself religious and yet does not keep a tight rein on his tongue, he deceives himself and his religion is worthless. Religion that God our Father accepts as pure and faultless is this: to look after orphans and widows in their distress and to keep oneself from being polluted by the world.

JAMES 1:26–27 NIV

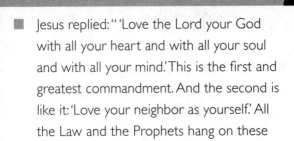

Jesus replied: " 'Love the Lord your God with all your heart and with all your soul and with all your mind.' This is the first and greatest commandment. And the second is like it: 'Love your neighbor as yourself.' All the Law and the Prophets hang on these two commandments."

MATTHEW 22:37–40 NIV

It's better to have a partner than go it alone.
Share the work, share the wealth.
And if one falls down, the other helps,
But if there's no one to help, tough!
Two in a bed warm each other.
Alone, you shiver all night.
By yourself you're unprotected.
With a friend you can face the worst.
Can you round up a third?
A three-stranded rope isn't easily snapped.

ECCLESIASTES 4:9–12 MSG

15

COMPASSION

▪ Be kind and compassionate to one
another, forgiving each other, just as
in Christ God forgave you.

EPHESIANS 4:32 NIV

▪ "Then the King will say to those on his right,
'Come, you who are blessed by my Father;
take your inheritance, the kingdom prepared
for you since the creation of the world. For
I was hungry and you gave me something to
eat, I was thirsty and you gave me something
to drink, I was a stranger and you invited me
in, I needed clothes and you clothed me,
I was sick and you looked after me, I was in
prison and you came to visit me.' . . .

   "The King will reply, 'I tell you the truth,
whatever you did for one of the least of
these brothers of mine, you did for me.' "

MATTHEW 25:34–40 NIV

■ Bear with each other and forgive whatever grievances you may have against one another. Forgive as the Lord forgave you. And over all these virtues put on love, which binds them all together in perfect unity.

COLOSSIANS 3:13–14 NIV

■ But you, O God, do see trouble and grief;
    you consider it to take it in hand.
The victim commits himself to you;
    you are the helper of the fatherless.

PSALM 10:14 NIV

■ A father to the fatherless, a defender of widows, is God in his holy dwelling.

PSALM 68:5 NIV

CONCERN

■ If there is a poor man among your brothers
in any of the towns of the land that the LORD
your God is giving you, do not be hardhearted
or tightfisted toward your poor brother.
Rather be openhanded and freely lend him
whatever he needs.

DEUTERONOMY 15:7–8 NIV

■ I'm glad in God, far happier than you would
ever guess—happy that you're again showing
such strong concern for me.

PHILIPPIANS 4:10 MSG

■ Share each other's burdens, and in this way
obey the law of Christ.

GALATIANS 6:2 NLT

■ If one part of our body hurts, we hurt all over. If one part of our body is honored, the whole body will be happy.

1 CORINTHIANS 12:26 CEV

■ "Take my yoke upon you and learn from me, for I am gentle and humble in heart, and you will find rest for your souls. For my yoke is easy and my burden is light."

MATTHEW 11:29–30 NIV

LONGING

■ A cheerful look brings joy to the heart,
and good news gives health to the bones.

PROVERBS 15:30 NIV

■ O LORD, be gracious to us;
    we long for you.
Be our strength every morning,
    our salvation in time of distress.

ISAIAH 33:2 NIV

■ So it is right that I should feel as I do about
all of you, for you have a special place in my
heart. You share with me the special favor
of God, both in my imprisonment and in
defending and confirming the truth of the
Good News.

PHILIPPIANS 1:7 NLT

Dear friends, I love you and long to see you.
Please keep on being faithful to the Lord.
You are my pride and joy.

PHILIPPIANS 4:1 CEV

LOVE

If I speak in the tongues of men and of angels, but have not love, I am only a resounding gong or a clanging cymbal. If I have the gift of prophecy and can fathom all mysteries and all knowledge, and if I have a faith that can move mountains, but have not love, I am nothing. If I give all I possess to the poor and surrender my body to the flames, but have not love, I gain nothing.

Love is patient, love is kind. It does not envy, it does not boast, it is not proud. It is not rude, it is not self-seeking, it is not easily angered, it keeps no record of wrongs. Love does not delight in evil but rejoices with the truth. It always protects, always trusts, always hopes, always perseveres.

Love never fails.

1 CORINTHIANS 13:1–8 NIV

■ One of the religion scholars came up. Hearing the lively exchanges of question and answer and seeing how sharp Jesus was in his answers, he put in his question: "Which is most important of all the commandments?"

Jesus said, "The first in importance is, 'Listen, Israel: The Lord your God is one; so love the Lord God with all your passion and prayer and intelligence and energy.' And here is the second: 'Love others as well as you love yourself.' There is no other commandment that ranks with these."

MARK 12:28–31 MSG

■ Such love has no fear, because perfect love expels all fear. If we are afraid, it is for fear of punishment, and this shows that we have not fully experienced his perfect love.

1 JOHN 4:18 NLT

■ "Greater love has no one than this, that he lay down his life for his friends."

JOHN 15:13 NIV

■ Above all, clothe yourselves with love, which binds us all together in perfect harmony. And let the peace that comes from Christ rule in your hearts. For as members of one body you are called to live in peace. And always be thankful.

COLOSSIANS 3:14–15 NLT

TENDERNESS

■ Is there any encouragement from belonging to Christ? Any comfort from his love? Any fellowship together in the Spirit? Are your hearts tender and compassionate? Then make me truly happy by agreeing wholeheartedly with each other, loving one another, and working together with one mind and purpose.

Don't be selfish; don't try to impress others. Be humble, thinking of others as better than yourselves. Don't look out only for your own interests, but take an interest in others, too.

You must have the same attitude that Christ Jesus had.

PHILIPPIANS 2:1–5 NLT

■ Finally, all of you should be of one mind. Sympathize with each other. Love each other as brothers and sisters. Be tenderhearted, and keep a humble attitude.

1 PETER 3:8 NLT

■ "Then the King will say, 'I'm telling the solemn truth: Whenever you did one of these things to someone overlooked or ignored, that was me—you did it to me.' "

MATTHEW 25:40 MSG

■ Since God chose you to be the holy people he loves, you must clothe yourselves with tenderhearted mercy, kindness, humility, gentleness, and patience.

COLOSSIANS 3:12 NLT

■ But the fruit of the Spirit is love, joy, peace, longsuffering, gentleness, goodness, faith, meekness, temperance: against such there is no law.

GALATIANS 5:22–23 KJV

ONE MOMENT
AT A TIME

ENJOYING LOVE

■ **Celebrate friendship.** Genuine love is a
hallmark of true friendships. Take time to
savor this precious gift. Invite a friend to go to
dinner or enjoy a weekend getaway. Let them
know how much you value and appreciate
the relationship that you share.

■ **Praise God.** God could have created people
to be stoic and free of emotion. Instead, He's
given us love partly so that we could better
understand the love He has for us. Praise
God for the love that He has shown you.

Be an agent of care. Almost everyone has something in their life that breaks their heart. For some, those moments are more regular and more present than others. Look for someone who is in need of some love and concern and find a way to encourage that person today.

CHAPTER 2

EMOTIONS OF JOY

I feel badly for people who don't take time to enjoy life. So many of my friends are too busy with work and the other stresses of life that they don't stop to enjoy the great things that happen each day. I have a couple of friends, in fact, that I haven't seen smile in a long time. It seems like when we get busy, the first thing to go is our joy. Somehow, I can't imagine that God intended for us to be so wrapped up in ourselves or our schedules that we can't take time to enjoy the life and world He's given us.

■ Ji Sun, age 31, Oregon ■

CHEERFULNESS

A happy heart makes the face cheerful,
but heartache crushes the spirit.

PROVERBS 15:13 NIV

A cheerful disposition is good for your health;
gloom and doom leave you bone-tired.

PROVERBS 17:22 MSG

O come, let us sing for joy to the LORD;
Let us shout joyfully to the rock of our
salvation.

PSALM 95:1 NASB

Make a joyful noise to the LORD, all the earth;
break forth into joyous song and sing praises!

PSALM 98:4 ESV

For the despondent, every day brings trouble;
for the happy heart, life is a continual feast.

PROVERBS 15:15 NLT

ENJOYMENT

So I commend the enjoyment of life, because nothing is better for a man under the sun than to eat and drink and be glad. Then joy will accompany him in his work all the days of the life God has given him under the sun.

ECCLESIASTES 8:15 NIV

And is there a man here who has planted a vineyard but hasn't yet enjoyed the grapes? Let him go home right now lest he die in battle and another man enjoy the grapes.

DEUTERONOMY 20:6 MSG

Nehemiah said, "Go and enjoy choice food and sweet drinks, and send some to those who have nothing prepared. This day is sacred to our Lord. Do not grieve, for the joy of the LORD is your strength.

NEHEMIAH 8:10 NIV

■ And it is a good thing to receive wealth from God and the good health to enjoy it. To enjoy your work and accept your lot in life—this is indeed a gift from God.

ECCLESIASTES 5:19 NLT

■ Even if you live a long time, don't take a single day for granted.
Take delight in each light-filled hour,
Remembering that there will also be many dark days
And that most of what comes your way is smoke.

ECCLESIASTES 11:8 MSG

■ [God] richly gives us all we need for our enjoyment.

1 TIMOTHY 6:17 NLT

ENTHUSIASM

■ Never be lacking in zeal, but keep your spiritual fervor, serving the Lord.

ROMANS 12:11 NIV

■ Whatever your hand finds to do, do it with all your might; for there is no activity or planning or knowledge or wisdom in Sheol where you are going.

ECCLESIASTES 9:10 NASB

■ It is not good to have zeal without knowledge, nor to be hasty and miss the way.

PROVERBS 19:2 NIV

■ And whatever you do, whether in word or deed, do it all in the name of the Lord Jesus, giving thanks to God the Father through him.

COLOSSIANS 3:17 NIV

GRATITUDE

■ Give thanks in all circumstances, for this is
God's will for you in Christ Jesus.

1 THESSALONIANS 5:18 NIV

■ Praise the LORD! Oh give thanks to the LORD,
for he is good, for his steadfast love
endures forever!

PSALM 106:1 ESV

■ Make thankfulness your sacrifice to God,
and keep the vows you made to the Most
High.

PSALM 50:14 NLT

■ What a beautiful thing, GOD, to give thanks,
to sing an anthem to you, the High God!

PSALM 92:1 MSG

Let us come into his presence with thanksgiving;
   let us make a joyful noise to him with songs
   of praise!
For the LORD is a great God,
   and a great King above all gods.

PSALM 95:2–3 ESV

Devote yourselves to prayer with an alert
mind and a thankful heart.

COLOSSIANS 4:2 NLT

Sing to the LORD!
   Praise the LORD!
For though I was poor and needy,
   he rescued me from my oppressors.

JEREMIAH 20:13 NLT

HAPPINESS

Let God All-Powerful
be your silver and gold,
and you will find happiness
by worshiping him.

JOB 22:25–26 CEV

May the LORD bless his people with peace
and happiness and let them celebrate.

PSALM 64:10 CEV

Wisdom makes life pleasant
and leads us safely along.
Wisdom is a life-giving tree,
the source of happiness
for all who hold on to her.

PROVERBS 3:17–18 CEV

Is any one of you in trouble? He should pray.
Is anyone happy? Let him sing songs of praise.

JAMES 5:13 NIV

■ You will come to know God even better. His glorious power will make you patient and strong enough to endure anything, and you will be truly happy.

COLOSSIANS 1:10–11 CEV

■ God's kingdom isn't about eating and drinking. It is about pleasing God, about living in peace, and about true happiness. All this comes from the Holy Spirit.

ROMANS 14:17 CEV

■ Happy are those who respect the Lord,
    who want what he commands.
Their descendants will be powerful in the
    land; the children of honest people will be
    blessed.

PSALM 112:1–2 NCV

■ I create light and darkness, happiness and sorrow. I, the Lord, do all of this.

ISAIAH 45:7 CEV

Happy are those who don't listen to the
    wicked, who don't go where sinners go,
    who don't do what evil people do.
They love the LORD's teachings, and they think
    about those teachings day and night.

PSALM 1:1–2 NCV

HOPE

■ Happy is he who has the God of Jacob for
   his help,
Whose hope is in the Lord his God.

PSALM 146:5 NKJV

■ May your unfailing love rest upon us, O Lord,
even as we put our hope in you.

PSALM 33:22 NIV

■ Why am I discouraged?
   Why is my heart so sad?
I will put my hope in God!
I will praise him again—
   my Savior and my God!

PSALM 42:11 NLT

■ I wait for the Lord, my soul waits,
And in His word I do hope.

PSALM 130:5 NKJV

Praise be to the God and Father of our Lord Jesus Christ! In his great mercy he has given us new birth into a living hope through the resurrection of Jesus Christ from the dead.

1 PETER 1:3 NIV

And this same God who takes care of me will supply all your needs from his glorious riches, which have been given to us in Christ Jesus.

PHILIPPIANS 4:19 NLT

For we know that when this earthly tent we live in is taken down (that is, when we die and leave this earthly body), we will have a house in heaven, an eternal body made for us by God himself and not by human hands.

2 CORINTHIANS 5:1 NLT

■ "For I know the plans I have for you," declares the LORD, "plans to prosper you and not to harm you, plans to give you hope and a future."

JEREMIAH 29:11 NIV

JOY

■ Be joyful in hope, patient in affliction, faithful in prayer.

ROMANS 12:12 NIV

■ You have put gladness in my heart,
  More than in the season that their grain
  and wine increased.

PSALM 4:7 NKJV

■ But the fruit of the Spirit is love, joy, peace, patience, kindness, goodness, faithfulness.

GALATIANS 5:22 NIV

■ Consider it pure joy, my brothers, whenever you face trials of many kinds, because you know that the testing of your faith develops perseverance. Perseverance must finish its work so that you may be mature and complete, not lacking anything.

JAMES 1:2–4 NIV

"Therefore you too have grief now; but I will see you again, and your heart will rejoice, and no one will take your joy away from you."

JOHN 16:22 NASB

Be full of joy in the Lord always. I will say again, be full of joy.

PHILIPPIANS 4:4 NCV

Though the fig tree does not bud
    and there are no grapes on the vines,
though the olive crop fails
    and the fields produce no food,
though there are no sheep in the pen
    and no cattle in the stalls,
yet I will rejoice in the LORD,
    I will be joyful in God my Savior.
The Sovereign LORD is my strength;
    he makes my feet like the feet of a deer,
    he enables me to go on the heights.

HABAKKUK 3:17–19 NIV

PLEASURE

■ A fool finds pleasure in evil conduct,
    but a man of understanding delights in
    wisdom.

PROVERBS 10:23 NIV

■ I will take pleasure in your laws and remember
your words.

PSALM 119:16 CEV

■ Do not love this world nor the things it offers
you, for when you love the world, you do
not have the love of the Father in you. For
the world offers only a craving for physical
pleasure, a craving for everything we see, and
pride in our achievements and possessions.
These are not from the Father, but are from
this world. And this world is fading away, along
with everything that people crave. But anyone
who does what pleases God will live forever.

1 JOHN 2:15–17 NLT

Seize life! ... Oh yes—God takes pleasure in your pleasure! Dress festively every morning. Don't skimp on colors and scarves.... Each day is God's gift.

ECCLESIASTES 9:7–9 MSG

TRIUMPH

With God's help we will do mighty things,
  for he will trample down our foes.

PSALM 108:13 NLT

For the LORD your God is the one who
goes with you to fight for you against your
enemies to give you victory.

DEUTERONOMY 20:4 NIV

"O Lord, let your ear be attentive to the
prayer of this your servant and to the prayer
of your servants who delight in revering your
name. Give your servant success today by
granting him favor in the presence of this man."

NEHEMIAH 1:11 NIV

You give me your shield of victory;
you stoop down to make me great.

2 SAMUEL 22:36 NIV

■ With the LORD on my side,
   I will defeat all of my hateful enemies.

PSALM 118:7 CEV

■ I am grateful that God always makes it possible for Christ to lead us to victory. God also helps us spread the knowledge about Christ everywhere, and this knowledge is like the smell of perfume.

2 CORINTHIANS 2:14 CEV

■ Count on this: The wicked won't get off scot-free, and God's loyal people will triumph.

PROVERBS 11:21 MSG

■ The horse is made ready for the day of battle,
   but victory rests with the LORD.

PROVERBS 21:31 NIV

WONDER

■ Let all that I am praise the LORD.
O LORD my God, how great you are!
You are robed with honor and majesty.
You are dressed in a robe of light.
You stretch out the starry curtain of the
heavens; you lay out the rafters of your
home in the rain clouds.
You make the clouds your chariot;
you ride upon the wings of the wind.
The winds are your messengers;
flames of fire are your servants. . . .
O LORD, what a variety of things you have
made!
In wisdom you have made them all.
The earth is full of your creatures.
Here is the ocean, vast and wide,
teeming with life of every kind,
both large and small.

PSALM 104:1–4, 24–25 NLT

O LORD, what is man that you care for him,
the son of man that you think of him?

PSALM 144:3 NIV

Who is like you, O LORD, among the gods?
Who is like you, majestic in holiness,
awesome in glorious deeds, doing wonders?

EXODUS 15:11 ESV

LORD, I have heard of your fame;
I stand in awe of your deeds, O LORD.
Renew them in our day,
in our time make them known;
in wrath remember mercy.

HABAKKUK 3:2 NIV

Our LORD and Ruler,
    your name is wonderful everywhere
    on earth!
You let your glory be seen
    in the heavens above....
I often think of the heavens
    your hands have made,
    and of the moon and stars
    you put in place.
Then I ask, "Why do you care
    about us humans?
Why are you concerned
    for us weaklings?"
You made us a little lower
    than you yourself,
    and you have crowned us
    with glory and honor.
You let us rule everything
    your hands have made.
And you put all of it
    under our power—
    the sheep and the cattle,

and every wild animal,
the birds in the sky,
the fish in the sea,
and all ocean creatures.
Our LORD and Ruler,
your name is wonderful
everywhere on earth!

PSALM 8:1–9 CEV

ONE MOMENT
AT A TIME

SHARE THE JOY

■ **Volunteer.** There are plenty of places filled
with hurting people that could use a warm
smile. Volunteer at a nursing home or soup
kitchen. Help out at a children's hospital.
Connect with a prison chaplain and ask if
there's an inmate who could use a visitor
or letter.

■ **Be positive.** Many people live in a constant
state of complaining. The weather is always
wrong, the traffic too heavy, and the stores
too crowded. Choose to look for the good in
every situation, and allow your positive out-
look to brighten up the world around you.

Write them down. God's blessings can be seen in both the good and the hard times of life. Create a journal where you write down what you're thankful for each day. Some days this may be easier to do than others, but if you're looking for it, you'll see God's goodness no matter your circumstances. When you find yourself growing discouraged, look back through your journal and remember all the reasons you have to rejoice.

CHAPTER 3

EMOTIONS OF PEACE

I love rock climbing. It's hard work and can be dangerous. There's not a day of climbing that goes by where my muscles don't ache and my skin doesn't get scraped. But while there's some pain associated with the sport, there's nothing like the feeling you have when you stand on top of the rock you've conquered. You look down and think to yourself, I made it! The thrill of the relief and satisfaction make the temporary pain worthwhile.

■ Ryan, age 27, Wyoming ■

COMFORT

Praise be to the God and Father of our Lord
Jesus Christ, the Father of compassion and
the God of all comfort, who comforts us
in all our troubles, so that we can comfort
those in any trouble with the comfort we
ourselves have received from God. For just
as the sufferings of Christ flow over into our
lives, so also through Christ our comfort
overflows.

2 CORINTHIANS 1:3–5 NIV

For this is what the LORD says:...
"As a mother comforts her child,
    so will I comfort you...."
When you see this, your heart will rejoice
    and you will flourish like grass;
the hand of the LORD will be made known
    to his servants,
but his fury will be shown to his foes.

ISAIAH 66:12–14 NIV

■ Even though I walk
   through the valley of the shadow of death,
I will fear no evil,
   for you are with me;
your rod and your staff,
   they comfort me.

PSALM 23:4 NIV

■ He comforts us in all our troubles so that we
can comfort others. When they are troubled,
we will be able to give them the same comfort God has given us.

2 CORINTHIANS 1:4 NLT

CONTENTMENT

■ Be still in the presence of the LORD,
  and wait patiently for him to act.
Don't worry about evil people who prosper
  or fret about their wicked schemes. . . .
It is better to be godly and have little
  than to be evil and rich.

PSALM 37:7, 16 NLT

■ "So do not worry, saying, 'What shall we
eat?' or 'What shall we drink?' or 'What shall
we wear?' For the pagans run after all these
things, and your heavenly Father knows that
you need them. But seek first his kingdom
and his righteousness, and all these things
will be given to you as well. Therefore do
not worry about tomorrow, for tomorrow
will worry about itself. Each day has enough
trouble of its own."

MATTHEW 6:31–34 NIV

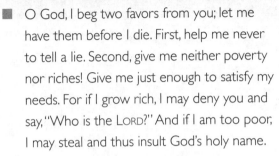

O God, I beg two favors from you; let me have them before I die. First, help me never to tell a lie. Second, give me neither poverty nor riches! Give me just enough to satisfy my needs. For if I grow rich, I may deny you and say, "Who is the LORD?" And if I am too poor, I may steal and thus insult God's holy name.

PROVERBS 30:7–9 NLT

I know what it is to be in need, and I know what it is to have plenty. I have learned the secret of being content in any and every situation, whether well fed or hungry, whether living in plenty or in want. I can do everything through him who gives me strength.

PHILIPPIANS 4:12–13 NIV

But if we have food and clothing, we will be content with that.

1 TIMOTHY 6:8 NIV

■ Yet true godliness with contentment is itself great wealth. After all, we brought nothing with us when we came into the world, and we can't take anything with us when we leave it.

1 TIMOTHY 6:6–7 NLT

PEACE

"I will heal my people and will let them enjoy abundant peace and security."

JEREMIAH 33:6 NIV

"I have told you these things, so that in me you may have peace. In this world you will have trouble. But take heart! I have overcome the world."

JOHN 16:33 NIV

Let the peace of Christ rule in your hearts, since as members of one body you were called to peace. And be thankful.

COLOSSIANS 3:15 NIV

"Peace I leave with you; my peace I give to you. Not as the world gives do I give to you. Let not your hearts be troubled, neither let them be afraid."

JOHN 14:27 ESV

You keep him in perfect peace
    whose mind is stayed on you,
    because he trusts in you.
Trust in the LORD forever,
    for the LORD GOD is an everlasting rock.

ISAIAH 26:3–4 ESV

Instead, pursue righteous living, faithfulness,
love, and peace. Enjoy the companionship of
those who call on the Lord with pure hearts.

2 TIMOTHY 2:22 NLT

"Though the mountains be shaken
    and the hills be removed,
yet my unfailing love for you will not be
    shaken nor my covenant of peace
    be removed,"
says the LORD, who has compassion on you.

ISAIAH 54:10 NIV

■ "Be still, and know that I am God;
I will be exalted among the nations,
I will be exalted in the earth."

PSALM 46:10 NIV

■ Since everything around us is going to be destroyed like this, what holy and godly lives you should live, looking forward to the day of God and hurrying it along. On that day, he will set the heavens on fire, and the elements will melt away in the flames. But we are looking forward to the new heavens and new earth he has promised, a world filled with God's righteousness.

And so, dear friends, while you are waiting for these things to happen, make every effort to be found living peaceful lives that are pure and blameless in his sight.

2 PETER 3:11–14 NLT

65

RELIEF

■ In my anguish I cried to the LORD,
    and he answered by setting me free.

PSALM 118:5 NIV

■ The LORD replied, "My Presence will go with
you, and I will give you rest."

EXODUS 33:14 NIV

■ When I felt my feet slipping,
    you came with your love and kept
    me steady.
And when I was burdened with worries,
    you comforted me and made me feel
    secure.

PSALM 94:18–19 CEV

■ Hear my prayer, O LORD;
    let my cry come to you!
Do not hide your face from me
    in the day of my distress!
Incline your ear to me;
    answer me speedily in the day when I call!

PSALM 102:1–2 ESV

■ I sought the LORD, and he answered me;
    he delivered me from all my fears.

PSALM 34:4 NIV

■ Blessed is the man you discipline, O LORD,
    the man you teach from your law;
you grant him relief from days of trouble,
    till a pit is dug for the wicked.

PSALM 94:12–13 NIV

SATISFACTION

▪ A man can do nothing better than to eat and drink and find satisfaction in his work. This too, I see, is from the hand of God.

ECCLESIASTES 2:24 NIV

▪ Yes, we should make the most of what God gives, both the bounty and the capacity to enjoy it, accepting what's given and delighting in the work. It's God's gift!

ECCLESIASTES 5:19 MSG

▪ Rejoice in the Lord always. I will say it again: Rejoice! Let your gentleness be evident to all. The Lord is near. Do not be anxious about anything, but in everything, by prayer and petition, with thanksgiving, present your requests to God. And the peace of God, which transcends all understanding, will guard your hearts and your minds in Christ Jesus.

PHILIPPIANS 4:4–7 NIV

Make it your ambition to lead a quiet life, to mind your own business and to work with your hands, just as we told you, so that your daily life may win the respect of outsiders and so that you will not be dependent on anybody.

1 THESSALONIANS 4:11–12 NIV

ONE MOMENT
AT A TIME

BE SATISFIED

■ **Take time.** Sometimes we're so busy crossing tasks off our list that we don't take time to enjoy life along the way. If that's the case with you, slow down enough to appreciate the good things God's given you today.

■ **Savor the happy times.** Take your family or friends to dinner or enjoy a trip together. Like a runner who takes a victory lap at the end of a race, savor the moments together. Write a prayer of thanks to God for these special times.

Create better habits. While stress is a useful tool and strong motivator, you should not live a life filled with 24/7 stress. Before long, you'll find yourself burning out. Carve out intervals for rest. Set aside time to relax with the people you love. Building in breaks along the way will help you live with a healthier balance.

CHAPTER 4

EMOTIONS OF PASSION

Our passions are gifts that exist on a razor's edge. One side is a healthy desire to get out of bed, conquer the world, and improve our lives. On the other side is a selfish ambition that consumes and can lead you to a path of sinful decisions. Passion unchecked can lead to unhealthy traits like greed, envy, or lust. Being able to distinguish between healthy motivation and sinful obsession is key to living a life that honors God.

■ Trent, age 57, Tennessee ■

AMBITION

▣ In his heart a man plans his course,
   but the LORD determines his steps.

   PROVERBS 16:9 NIV

▣ Everything comes from the Lord. All things
   were made because of him and will return to
   him. Praise the Lord forever! Amen.

   ROMANS 11:36 CEV

▣ "I own the silver, I own the gold," decrees
   [God].

   HAGGAI 2:8 MSG

▣ The blessing of the LORD makes a person rich,
   and he adds no sorrow with it.

   PROVERBS 10:22 NLT

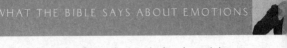

■ The desires of good people lead straight
   to the best,
but wicked ambition ends in angry frustration.

PROVERBS 11:23 MSG

■ Submit to God and be at peace with him;
   in this way prosperity will come to you.

JOB 22:21 NIV

COURAGE

So whenever we are in need, we should come bravely before the throne of our merciful God. There we will be treated with undeserved kindness, and we will find help.

HEBREWS 4:16 CEV

Be brave and strong! Don't be afraid. . . . The LORD your God will always be at your side, and he will never abandon you.

DEUTERONOMY 31:6 CEV

The high and lofty one who lives in eternity, the Holy One, says this:
"I live in the high and holy place with those whose spirits are contrite and humble.
I restore the crushed spirit of the humble and revive the courage of those with repentant hearts."

ISAIAH 57:15 NLT

"Have I not commanded you? Be strong and courageous. Do not be terrified; do not be discouraged, for the LORD your God will be with you wherever you go."

JOSHUA 1:9 NIV

DESIRE

■ Instead, clothe yourself with the presence of the Lord Jesus Christ. And don't let yourself think about ways to indulge your evil desires.

ROMANS 13:14 NLT

■ Put to death, therefore, whatever belongs to your earthly nature: sexual immorality, impurity, lust, evil desires and greed, which is idolatry.

COLOSSIANS 3:5 NIV

■ For everything in the world—the cravings of sinful man, the lust of his eyes and the boasting of what he has and does—comes not from the Father but from the world.

1 JOHN 2:16 NIV

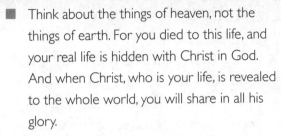

Think about the things of heaven, not the things of earth. For you died to this life, and your real life is hidden with Christ in God. And when Christ, who is your life, is revealed to the whole world, you will share in all his glory.

COLOSSIANS 3:2–4 NLT

The righteousness of the upright delivers them, but the unfaithful are trapped by evil desires.

PROVERBS 11:6 NIV

DETERMINATION

■ To this end we always pray for you, that our God may make you worthy of his calling and may fulfill every resolve for good and every work of faith by his power, so that the name of our Lord Jesus may be glorified in you, and you in him, according to the grace of our God and the Lord Jesus Christ.

2 THESSALONIANS 1:11–12 ESV

■ Therefore, I urge you, brothers, in view of God's mercy, to offer your bodies as living sacrifices, holy and pleasing to God—this is your spiritual act of worship. Do not conform any longer to the pattern of this world, but be transformed by the renewing of your mind. Then you will be able to test and ap-prove what God's will is—his good, pleasing and perfect will.

ROMANS 12:1–2 NIV

■ "Suppose one of you wants to build a tower. Will he not first sit down and estimate the cost to see if he has enough money to complete it? For if he lays the foundation and is not able to finish it, everyone who sees it will ridicule him, saying, 'This fellow began to build and was not able to finish.' "

LUKE 14:28–30 NIV

■ Finishing is better than starting.
   Patience is better than pride.

ECCLESIASTES 7:8 NLT

■ God blesses those who patiently endure testing and temptation. Afterward they will receive the crown of life that God has promised to those who love him. And remember, when you are being tempted, do not say, "God is tempting me." God is never tempted to do wrong, and he never tempts anyone else.

JAMES 1:12–13 NLT

81

Because the Sovereign Lord helps me,
    I will not be disgraced.
Therefore, I have set my face like a stone,
    determined to do his will.
And I know that I will not be put to shame.
He who gives me justice is near.
    Who will dare to bring charges against
    me now?
Where are my accusers?
    Let them appear!
See, the Sovereign Lord is on my side!
    Who will declare me guilty?
All my enemies will be destroyed
    like old clothes that have been eaten by
    moths!

Isaiah 50:7–9 NLT

ENVY

Then I observed that most people are motivated to success because they envy their neighbors. But this, too, is meaningless—like chasing the wind.

ECCLESIASTES 4:4 NLT

Whenever people are jealous or selfish, they cause trouble and do all sorts of cruel things.

JAMES 3:16 CEV

You want what you don't have, so you scheme and kill to get it. You are jealous of what others have, but you can't get it, so you fight and wage war to take it away from them. Yet you don't have what you want because you don't ask God for it. And even when you ask, you don't get it because your motives are all wrong—you want only what will give you pleasure.

JAMES 4:2–3 NLT

83

It's healthy to be content, but envy can eat you up.

PROVERBS 14:30 CEV

Let us not become conceited, provoking and envying each other.

GALATIANS 5:26 NIV

GREED

■ Greed causes fighting;
   trusting the LORD leads to prosperity.

PROVERBS 28:25 NLT

■ Whoever loves money never has money
   enough; whoever loves wealth is never
   satisfied with his income. This too is
   meaningless.

ECCLESIASTES 5:10 NIV

■ "Watch out! Be on your guard against all
   kinds of greed; a man's life does not consist
   in the abundance of his possessions."

LUKE 12:15 NIV

■ The trustworthy person will get a rich reward, but a person who wants quick riches will get into trouble.

PROVERBS 28:20 NLT

■ But people who long to be rich fall into temptation and are trapped by many foolish and harmful desires that plunge them into ruin and destruction.

1 TIMOTHY 6:9 NLT

INFATUATION

Above all else, guard your heart,
   for it is the wellspring of life.

PROVERBS 4:23 NIV

Do not lust in your heart after her beauty
   or let her captivate you with her eyes,
   for the prostitute reduces you to a loaf of
   bread, and the adulteress preys upon your
   very life.
Can a man scoop fire into his lap
   without his clothes being burned?
Can a man walk on hot coals
   without his feet being scorched?
So is he who sleeps with another man's wife;
   no one who touches her will go
   unpunished.

PROVERBS 6:25–29 NIV

■ I saw some naive young men, and one in
  particular who lacked common sense.

He was crossing the street near the house of
  an immoral woman, strolling down the path
  by her house....

She threw her arms around him and kissed
  him, and with a brazen look she said, ...

"Come, let's drink our fill of love until morning.

Let's enjoy each other's caresses,
  for my husband is not home.

He's away on a long trip...."

So she seduced him with her pretty speech
  and enticed him with her flattery....

He was like a bird flying into a snare,
  little knowing it would cost him his life.

So listen to me, my sons,
  and pay attention to my words.

Don't let your hearts stray away toward her.

Don't wander down her wayward path.

For she has been the ruin of many;
  many men have been her victims.

PROVERBS 7:7–26 NLT

LUST

■ God has called us to live holy lives, not impure lives.

1 THESSALONIANS 4:7 NLT

■ "But I tell you that anyone who looks at a woman lustfully has already committed adultery with her in his heart."

MATTHEW 5:28 NIV

■ Let us behave decently, as in the daytime, not in orgies and drunkenness, not in sexual immorality and debauchery, not in dissension and jealousy.

ROMANS 13:13 NIV

■ Run from anything that stimulates youthful lusts. Instead, pursue righteous living, faithfulness, love, and peace.

2 TIMOTHY 2:22 NLT

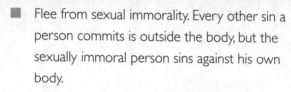

■ Flee from sexual immorality. Every other sin a person commits is outside the body, but the sexually immoral person sins against his own body.

1 CORINTHIANS 6:18 ESV

■ Let there be no sexual immorality, impurity, or greed among you. Such sins have no place among God's people.

EPHESIANS 5:3 NLT

■ "I made a covenant with my eyes not to look lustfully at a girl."

JOB 31:1 NIV

PASSION

■ Don't you realize that your body is the temple of the Holy Spirit, who lives in you and was given to you by God? You do not belong to yourself, for God bought you with a high price. So you must honor God with your body.

1 CORINTHIANS 6:19–20 NLT

■ So whether you eat or drink or whatever you do, do it all for the glory of God.

1 CORINTHIANS 10:31 NIV

■ For the grace of God that brings salvation has appeared to all men. It teaches us to say "No" to ungodliness and worldly passions, and to live self-controlled, upright and godly lives in this present age.

TITUS 2:11–12 NIV

■ Delight yourself in the LORD and he will give you the desires of your heart.

PSALM 37:4 NIV

■ Place me like a seal over your heart, like a seal on your arm; for love is as strong as death, its jealousy unyielding as the grave. It burns like blazing fire, like a mighty flame. Many waters cannot quench love; rivers cannot wash it away. If one were to give all the wealth of his house for love, it would be utterly scorned.

SONG OF SOLOMON 8:6–7 NIV

PLAYFULNESS

■ There is a time for everything,
and a season for every activity under heaven:
a time to be born and a time to die,
a time to plant and a time to uproot,
a time to kill and a time to heal,
a time to tear down and a time to build,
a time to weep and a time to laugh,
a time to mourn and a time to dance.

ECCLESIASTES 3:1–4 NIV

■ Relish life with the spouse you love
Each and every day of your precarious life.
Each day is God's gift. It's all you get in
exchange
For the hard work of staying alive.
Make the most of each one!

ECCLESIASTES 9:9 MSG

■ You who are young, make the most of your
   youth.
   Relish your youthful vigor.
   Follow the impulses of your heart.
   If something looks good to you, pursue it.
   But know also that not just anything goes;
   You have to answer to God for every last bit
   of it.

                                ECCLESIASTES 11:9 MSG

■ On your feet now—applaud GOD! Bring a gift
   of laughter, sing yourselves into his presence.

                                PSALM 100:1 MSG

PRIDE

■ Too much pride causes trouble. Be sensible
and take advice.

PROVERBS 13:10 CEV

■ To fear the LORD is to hate evil;
I hate pride and arrogance,
evil behavior and perverse speech.

PROVERBS 8:13 NIV

■ Pride goes before destruction,
a haughty spirit before a fall.

PROVERBS 16:18 NIV

■ Too much pride can put you to shame.
It's wiser to be humble.

PROVERBS 11:2 CEV

ONE MOMENT
AT A TIME

LIVING
PASSIONATELY

- **Separate the good from the bad.** Examine the desires you have and evaluate where healthy desires may be crossing into destructive behaviors. Ask God to help you refocus your passions into channels that honor Him.

- **Enlist help.** Just sharing your struggles with someone who cares will help you keep them in perspective. Share with a family member or friend and ask them to hold you accountable so that you don't let areas of weakness get the best of you.

Memorize Romans 12:1–2. Commit this verse to memory and then determine to live it out. Every day you have the opportunity to choose to offer your passions to God as an act of worship.

CHAPTER 5

EMOTIONS OF ANGER

No one makes me as angry as my extended family! They set up unreasonable expectations and hold me to standards that I have no way of meeting. And sure enough, I feel the sting of their criticism when I don't live up to what they have in mind. Hardly a week goes by when I'm not given a guilt trip or a lecture letting me in on yet another way I've let them down. Sometimes I just want to move out of state and get away from this craziness—at least then the anger wouldn't come bubbling up so quickly. But as soon as I start fantasizing about running away, I realize that there must be a better way.

■ Shandrice, age 34, Connecticut ■

ANGER

■ A gentle answer turns away wrath,
But a harsh word stirs up anger.

PROVERBS 15:1 NASB

■ "In your anger do not sin:" Do not let the sun
go down while you are still angry.

EPHESIANS 4:26 NIV

■ Human anger does not produce the righteousness God desires.

JAMES 1:20 NLT

■ Don't befriend angry people
or associate with hot-tempered people,
or you will learn to be like them
and endanger your soul.

PROVERBS 22:24–25 NLT

■ Better to be patient than powerful;
   better to have self-control than to conquer
   a city.

PROVERBS 16:32 NLT

■ Using good sense can put out the flames of
anger.

PROVERBS 29:8 CEV

BITTERNESS

■ Keep a sharp eye out for weeds of bitter discontent. A thistle or two gone to seed can ruin a whole garden in no time.

HEBREWS 12:15 MSG

■ Let all bitterness and wrath and anger and clamor and slander be put away from you, along with all malice.

EPHESIANS 4:31 ESV

■ Above all else, guard your heart,
for it is the wellspring of life.

PROVERBS 4:23 NIV

■ But when you are praying, first forgive anyone you are holding a grudge against, so that your Father in heaven will forgive your sins, too.

MARK 11:25 NLT

■ Dear friends, let us continue to love one another, for love comes from God. Anyone who loves is a child of God and knows God. But anyone who does not love does not know God, for God is love.

1 JOHN 4:7–8 NLT

■ Be patient and trust the LORD. Don't let it bother you when all goes well for those who do sinful things.
Don't be angry or furious. Anger can lead to sin.

PSALM 37:7–8 CEV

■ Then Peter came to Jesus and asked, "Lord, how many times shall I forgive my brother when he sins against me? Up to seven times?"
Jesus answered, "I tell you, not seven times, but seventy-seven times."

MATTHEW 18:21–22 NIV

CONTEMPT

■ When wickedness arrives, shame's not far behind; contempt for life is contemptible.

PROVERBS 18:3 MSG

■ But love your enemies, do good to them, and lend to them without expecting to get anything back. Then your reward will be great, and you will be sons of the Most High, because he is kind to the ungrateful and wicked. Be merciful, just as your Father is merciful.

Do not judge, and you will not be judged. Do not condemn, and you will not be condemned. Forgive, and you will be forgiven. Give, and it will be given to you. A good measure, pressed down, shaken together and running over, will be poured into your lap. For with the measure you use, it will be measured to you.

LUKE 6:35–38 NIV

"I'm telling you that anyone who is so much as angry with a brother or sister is guilty of murder. Carelessly call a brother 'idiot!' and you just might find yourself hauled into court. Thoughtlessly yell 'stupid!' at a sister and you are on the brink of hellfire. The simple moral fact is that words kill."

MATTHEW 5:22 MSG

FRUSTRATION

■ And he passed in front of Moses, proclaiming,
"The LORD, the LORD, the compassionate and
gracious God, slow to anger, abounding in
love and faithfulness."

EXODUS 34:6 NIV

■ We grow weary in our present bodies,
and we long to put on our heavenly bodies
like new clothing. . . . While we live in these
earthly bodies, we groan and sigh, but it's
not that we want to die and get rid of these
bodies that clothe us. Rather, we want to
put on our new bodies so that these dying
bodies will be swallowed up by life.

2 CORINTHIANS 5:2, 4 NLT

For the creation was subjected to frustration, not by its own choice, but by the will of the one who subjected it, in hope that the creation itself will be liberated from its bondage to decay and brought into the glorious freedom of the children of God.

We know that the whole creation has been groaning as in the pains of childbirth right up to the present time. . . .

In the same way, the Spirit helps us in our weakness. We do not know what we ought to pray for, but the Spirit himself intercedes for us with groans that words cannot express.

ROMANS 8:20–26 NIV

God, you're my last chance of the day.
I spend the night on my knees before you.
Put me on your salvation agenda;
   take notes on the trouble I'm in.
I've had my fill of trouble;
   I'm camped on the edge of hell.
I'm written off as a lost cause,
   one more statistic, a hopeless case.
Abandoned as already dead,
   one more body in a stack of corpses,
And not so much as a gravestone—
   I'm a black hole in oblivion.
You've dropped me into a bottomless pit,
   sunk me in a pitch-black abyss.
I'm battered senseless by your rage,
   relentlessly pounded by your waves of anger.
You turned my friends against me,
   made me horrible to them.
I'm caught in a maze and can't find my way out,
   blinded by tears of pain and frustration.

PSALM 88:1–9 MSG

HATE

■ Only fools get angry quickly and hold a
grudge.

ECCLESIASTES 7:9 CEV

■ But now you must stop doing such things.
You must quit being angry, hateful, and evil.
You must no longer say insulting or cruel
things about others.

COLOSSIANS 3:8 CEV

■ Anyone who claims to be in the light but
hates his brother is still in the darkness.
Whoever loves his brother lives in the light,
and there is nothing in him to make him
stumble. But whoever hates his brother is in
the darkness and walks around in the darkness; he does not know where he is going,
because the darkness has blinded him.

1 JOHN 2:9–11 NIV

People may cover their hatred with pleasant
    words, but they're deceiving you.
They pretend to be kind, but don't believe
    them.
Their hearts are full of many evils.
While their hatred may be concealed by
    trickery, their wrongdoing will be exposed
    in public.

PROVERBS 26:24–26 NLT

"'Do not hate your brother in your heart.
Rebuke your neighbor frankly so you will not
share in his guilt.'"

LEVITICUS 19:17 NIV

Bear with each other and forgive whatever
grievances you may have against one another.
Forgive as the Lord forgave you.

COLOSSIANS 3:13 NIV

HOSTILITY

■ "Blessed are those who are persecuted because of righteousness, for theirs is the kingdom of heaven.

Blessed are you when people insult you, persecute you and falsely say all kinds of evil against you because of me. Rejoice and be glad, because great is your reward in heaven, for in the same way they persecuted the prophets who were before you."

MATTHEW 5:10–12 NIV

■ Don't be angry or furious. Anger can lead to sin.

PSALM 37:8 CEV

■ "But I tell you: Love your enemies and pray for those who persecute you."

MATTHEW 5:44 NIV

If you see your enemy hungry, go buy him
lunch; if he's thirsty, bring him a drink.
Your generosity will surprise him with
goodness, and GOD will look after you.

PROVERBS 25:21–22 MSG

IRRITATION

■ Don't be quick to fly off the handle.
Anger boomerangs. You can spot a fool by
the lumps on his head.

ECCLESIASTES 7:9 MSG

■ Don't grumble against each other, brothers,
or you will be judged. The Judge is standing at
the door!

JAMES 5:9 NIV

■ Fools have short fuses and explode all too
quickly; the prudent quietly shrug off insults.

PROVERBS 12:16 MSG

■ My dear brothers, take note of this: Everyone
should be quick to listen, slow to speak and
slow to become angry.

JAMES 1:19 NIV

A hot-tempered person starts fights;
   a cool-tempered person stops them.

PROVERBS 15:18 NLT

It makes a lot of sense to be a person of few
words and to stay calm.

PROVERBS 17:27 CEV

VENGEFULNESS

Beloved, never avenge yourselves, but leave
it to the wrath of God, for it is written,
"Vengeance is mine, I will repay, says the
Lord." To the contrary, "if your enemy is
hungry, feed him; if he is thirsty, give him
something to drink; for by so doing you
will heap burning coals on his head." Do
not be overcome by evil, but overcome evil
with good.

ROMANS 12:19–21 ESV

People insulted Christ, but he did not insult
them in return. Christ suffered, but he did not
threaten. He let God, the One who judges
rightly, take care of him.

1 PETER 2:23 NCV

■ You shall not take vengeance or bear a
grudge against the sons of your own people,
but you shall love your neighbor as yourself:
I am the LORD.

LEVITICUS 19:18 ESV

■ Don't say, "I'll get even;
    I'll do to him what he did to me."

PROVERBS 24:29 NCV

■ Make sure that nobody pays back wrong
for wrong, but always try to be kind to each
other and to everyone else.

1 THESSALONIANS 5:15 NIV

■ It is a righteous thing with God to repay with tribulation those who trouble you.

2 THESSALONIANS 1:6 NKJV

■ For we know him that hath said, Vengeance belongeth unto me, I will recompense, saith the Lord.

HEBREWS 10:30 KJV

■ O LORD, the God of vengeance, O God of vengeance, let your glorious justice shine forth!

PSALM 94:1 NLT

ONE MOMENT
AT A TIME

DEALING WITH
ANGER

- **Prepare to be provoked.** If certain people or situations set you off, then learn to anticipate those times. Prepare yourself in advance so that you don't find yourself giving in to anger so quickly.

- **Don't assume the worst.** Once tensions are high, it's easy to read harsh motivations into every action or word. Try to take a step back and believe the best intentions of others.

Don't be a casualty. Living with chronic anger or bitterness creates an unexpected victim: you.

CHAPTER 6

EMOTIONS OF SADNESS

I was unprepared for the flood of emotions that swept over me when I lost my job. Before it happened, I thought my job was just a means for income. But since I've been laid off, I've suffered from feelings of rejection, discouragement, defeat, and shame. I don't even want to get out of bed and look for a new job. Being crippled by my emotions is a completely new experience for me. I feel like I'm drowning, and I'm not sure how much longer I can keep my nose above water.

■ Quincy, age 41, Delaware ■

BOREDOM

■ Go to work in the morning
   and stick to it until evening without
   watching the clock.
You never know from moment to moment
   how your work will turn out in the end.

ECCLESIASTES 11:6 MSG

■ Lazy hands make a man poor,
   but diligent hands bring wealth.

PROVERBS 10:4 NIV

■ In the name of the Lord Jesus Christ,
we command you, brothers, to keep away
from every brother who is idle and does
not live according to the teaching you
received from us.

2 THESSALONIANS 3:6 NIV

A shiftless man lives in a tumbledown shack;
A lazy woman ends up with a leaky roof.

ECCLESIASTES 10:18 MSG

We urge you, brothers, warn those who are idle, encourage the timid, help the weak, be patient with everyone.

1 THESSALONIANS 5:14 NIV

CONFUSION

■ And you will know the truth, and the truth
will set you free.

JOHN 8:32 NLT

■ Direct my footsteps according to your word;
let no sin rule over me.

PSALM 119:133 NIV

■ Whether you turn to the right or to the left,
your ears will hear a voice behind you, saying,
"This is the way; walk in it."

ISAIAH 30:21 NIV

■ Lead me in the right path, O LORD,
or my enemies will conquer me.
Make your way plain for me to follow.

PSALM 5:8 NLT

For this God is our God for ever and ever;
  he will be our guide even to the end.

PSALM 48:14 NIV

Lady Wisdom goes to town, stands in a prominent place, and invites everyone within sound of her voice:

  "Are you confused about life, don't know what's going on?

  Come with me, oh come, have dinner with me!

  I've prepared a wonderful spread—fresh-baked bread, roast lamb, carefully selected wines.

  Leave your impoverished confusion and live!

  Walk up the street to a life with meaning."

PROVERBS 9:3–6 MSG

DEFEAT

■ Now to him who is able to keep you from stumbling and to present you blameless before the presence of his glory with great joy, to the only God, our Savior, through Jesus Christ our Lord, be glory, majesty, dominion, and authority, before all time and now and forever. Amen.

JUDE 24–25 ESV

■ "The LORD himself will fight for you. Just stay calm."

EXODUS 14:14 NLT

■ Trust in him at all times, O people;
  pour out your hearts to him,
    for God is our refuge.

PSALM 62:8 NIV

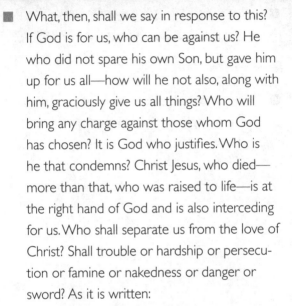

What, then, shall we say in response to this? If God is for us, who can be against us? He who did not spare his own Son, but gave him up for us all—how will he not also, along with him, graciously give us all things? Who will bring any charge against those whom God has chosen? It is God who justifies. Who is he that condemns? Christ Jesus, who died— more than that, who was raised to life—is at the right hand of God and is also interceding for us. Who shall separate us from the love of Christ? Shall trouble or hardship or persecution or famine or nakedness or danger or sword? As it is written:

"For your sake we face death all day long; we are considered as sheep to be slaughtered."

No, in all these things we are more than conquerors through him who loved us.

ROMANS 8:31–37 NIV

127

■ [God] redeems your life from the pit
  and crowns you with love and compassion.

PSALM 103:4 NIV

■ "For I know the plans I have for you," declares
  the LORD, "plans to prosper you and not
  to harm you, plans to give you hope and a
  future."

JEREMIAH 29:11 NIV

DEPRESSION

■ The Lord your God is with you,
    he is mighty to save.
He will take great delight in you,
    he will quiet you with his love,
    he will rejoice over you with singing.

ZEPHANIAH 3:17 NIV

■ I waited patiently for the Lord to help me,
    and he turned to me and heard
    my cry.
He lifted me out of the pit of despair,
    out of the mud and the mire.
He set my feet on solid ground
    and steadied me as I walked along.

PSALM 40:1–2 NLT

■ The LORD is close to the brokenhearted;
    he rescues those whose spirits are crushed.

PSALM 34:18 NLT

■ I lift my hands to you in prayer.
I thirst for you as parched land thirsts for rain.
Come quickly, LORD, and answer me,
    for my depression deepens.
Don't turn away from me,
    or I will die.
Let me hear of your unfailing love each
    morning, for I am trusting you.
Show me where to walk,
    for I give myself to you.

PSALM 143:6–8 NLT

■ I have received such wonderful revelations from God. So to keep me from becoming proud, I was given a thorn in my flesh, a messenger from Satan to torment me and keep me from becoming proud.

Three different times I begged the Lord to take it away. Each time he said, "My grace is all you need. My power works best in weakness." So now I am glad to boast about my weaknesses, so that the power of Christ can work through me.

2 CORINTHIANS 12:7–9 NLT

DISCOURAGEMENT

Why am I discouraged?
Why am I restless? I trust you!
And I will praise you again because you
help me.

PSALM 42:5 CEV

The LORD himself goes before you and will be
with you; he will never leave you nor forsake
you. Do not be afraid; do not be discouraged.

DEUTERONOMY 31:8 NIV

"Do not be afraid or discouraged because of
this vast army. For the battle is not yours,
but God's."

2 CHRONICLES 20:15 NIV

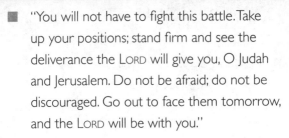

■ "You will not have to fight this battle. Take
up your positions; stand firm and see the
deliverance the LORD will give you, O Judah
and Jerusalem. Do not be afraid; do not be
discouraged. Go out to face them tomorrow,
and the LORD will be with you."

2 CHRONICLES 20:17 NIV

■ He heals the brokenhearted
and binds up their wounds.

PSALM 147:3 NIV

■ May our Lord Jesus Christ himself and God
our Father, who loved us and by his grace
gave us eternal encouragement and good
hope, encourage your hearts and strengthen
you in every good deed and word.

2 THESSALONIANS 2:16–17 NIV

EMBARRASSMENT

▪ In you, O LORD, do I take refuge;
let me never be put to shame!

PSALM 71:1 ESV

▪ He has never let you down,
never looked the other way when you
were being kicked around.
He has never wandered off to do his
own thing; he has been right there,
listening.

PSALM 22:24 MSG

▪ For God gave us a spirit not of fear but of
power and love and self-control.

2 TIMOTHY 1:7 ESV

■ Great is his faithfulness;
   his mercies begin afresh each morning.
I say to myself, "The LORD is my inheritance;
   therefore, I will hope in him!"

LAMENTATIONS 3:23–24 NLT

■ The LORD is good,
   a refuge in times of trouble.
He cares for those who trust in him.

NAHUM 1:7 NIV

■ Let us fix our eyes on Jesus, the author
and perfecter of our faith, who for the joy
set before him endured the cross, scorn-
ing its shame, and sat down at the right
hand of the throne of God. Consider him
who endured such opposition from sinful
men, so that you will not grow weary and
lose heart.

HEBREWS 12:2–3 NIV

EMPTINESS

How great is the love the Father has lavished on us, that we should be called children of God! And that is what we are! The reason the world does not know us is that it did not know him.

1 JOHN 3:1 NIV

How precious are your thoughts about me,
    O God.
They cannot be numbered!
I can't even count them;
    they outnumber the grains of sand!
And when I wake up,
    you are still with me!

PSALM 139:17–18 NLT

"What is the price of five sparrows—two copper coins? Yet God does not forget a single one of them. And the very hairs on your head are all numbered. So don't be afraid; you are more valuable to God than a whole flock of sparrows."

LUKE 12:6–7 NLT

"The thief comes only to steal and kill and destroy; I have come that they may have life, and have it to the full."

JOHN 10:10 NIV

For he will command his angels concerning you to guard you in all your ways.

PSALM 91:11 NIV

"Your Father knows exactly what you need even before you ask him!"

MATTHEW 6:8 NLT

GRIEF

People are born for trouble
as readily as sparks fly up from a fire.

JOB 5:7 NLT

I'm still in your presence,
but you've taken my hand.
You wisely and tenderly lead me,
and then you bless me.

PSALM 73:23–24 MSG

"Naked I came from my mother's womb,
and naked I will depart.
The LORD gave and the LORD has taken away;
may the name of the LORD be praised."

JOB 1:21 NIV

What I am saying, dear brothers and sisters, is that our physical bodies cannot inherit the Kingdom of God. These dying bodies cannot inherit what will last forever.

But let me reveal to you a wonderful secret. We will not all die, but we will all be transformed! It will happen in a moment, in the blink of an eye, when the last trumpet is blown. For when the trumpet sounds, those who have died will be raised to live forever. And we who are living will also be transformed. For our dying bodies must be transformed into bodies that will never die; our mortal bodies must be transformed into immortal bodies.

Then, when our dying bodies have been transformed into bodies that will never die, this Scripture will be fulfilled:

"Death is swallowed up in victory.
O death, where is your victory?
O death, where is your sting?"

1 CORINTHIANS 15:50–55 NLT

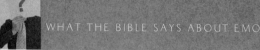

■ My friends, we want you to understand how it will be for those followers who have already died. Then you won't grieve over them and be like people who don't have any hope. We believe that Jesus died and was raised to life. We also believe that when God brings Jesus back again, he will bring with him all who had faith in Jesus before they died.

1 THESSALONIANS 4:13–14 CEV

■ I saw a new heaven and a new earth.... I heard a loud voice shout from the throne: God's home is now with his people. He will live with them, and they will be his own. Yes, God will make his home among his people. He will wipe all tears from their eyes, and there will be no more death, suffering, crying, or pain. These things of the past are gone forever.

REVELATION 21:1–4 CEV

■ You don't need to cry anymore. The Lord is
kind, and as soon as he hears your cries for
help, he will come.

ISAIAH 30:19 CEV

GUILT

■ If we confess our sins, he is faithful and just and will forgive us our sins and purify us from all unrighteousness.

1 JOHN 1:9 NIV

■ I—yes, I alone—will blot out your sins for my own sake and will never think of them again.

ISAIAH 43:25 NLT

■ Don't stay far away, LORD!
My strength comes from you, so hurry
    and help.
Rescue me from enemy swords
    and save me from those dogs.
Don't let lions eat me.
You rescued me from the horns of wild bulls.

PSALM 22:19–21 CEV

Anyone who belongs to Christ has become a new person. The old life is gone; a new life has begun!

And all of this is a gift from God, who brought us back to himself through Christ. And God has given us this task of reconciling people to him. For God was in Christ, reconciling the world to himself, no longer counting people's sins against them. And he gave us this wonderful message of reconciliation. So we are Christ's ambassadors; God is making his appeal through us. We speak for Christ when we plead, "Come back to God!" For God made Christ, who never sinned, to be the offering for our sin, so that we could be made right with God through Christ.

2 CORINTHIANS 5:17–21 NLT

■ As far as the east is from the west, so far does he remove our transgressions from us.

PSALM 103:12 ESV

■ Therefore, there is now no condemnation for those who are in Christ Jesus, because through Christ Jesus the law of the Spirit of life set me free from the law of sin and death.

ROMANS 8:1–2 NIV

HOPELESSNESS

Being confident of this, that he who began
a good work in you will carry it on to
completion until the day of Christ Jesus.

PHILIPPIANS 1:6 NIV

LORD, you know the hopes of the helpless.
Surely you will hear their cries and comfort
them.

PSALM 10:17 NLT

"But I will restore you to health and heal
your wounds," declares the LORD,
"because you are called an outcast,
Zion for whom no one cares."

JEREMIAH 30:17 NIV

Do you not know?
  Have you not heard?
The Lord is the everlasting God,
  the Creator of the ends of the earth.
He will not grow tired or weary,
  and his understanding no one can fathom.
He gives strength to the weary
  and increases the power of the weak.
Even youths grow tired and weary,
  and young men stumble and fall;
but those who hope in the Lord
  will renew their strength.
They will soar on wings like eagles;
  they will run and not grow weary,
  they will walk and not be faint.

ISAIAH 40:28–31 NIV

■ For our citizenship is in heaven, from which also we eagerly wait for a Savior, the Lord Jesus Christ.

PHILIPPIANS 3:20 NASB

■ For you have been my hope, O Sovereign LORD, my confidence since my youth.

PSALM 71:5 NIV

LONELINESS

■ The LORD your God will always be at your
side, and he will never abandon you.

DEUTERONOMY 31:6 CEV

■ Turn to me and be gracious to me,
for I am lonely and afflicted.

PSALM 25:16 NIV

■ Do you have any idea how very homesick we
became for you, dear friends? Even though
it hadn't been that long and it was only our
bodies that were separated from you, not
our hearts, we tried our very best to get
back to see you.

1 THESSALONIANS 2:17 MSG

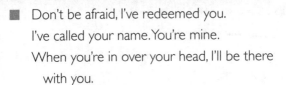

Don't be afraid, I've redeemed you.
I've called your name. You're mine.
When you're in over your head, I'll be there
  with you.
When you're in rough waters, you will not
  go down.
When you're between a rock and a hard
  place, it won't be a dead end—
Because I am God, your personal God,
  The Holy of Israel, your Savior.
I paid a huge price for you: all of Egypt,
  with rich Cush and Seba thrown in!
That's how much you mean to me!
That's how much I love you!
I'd sell off the whole world to get you back,
  trade the creation just for you.

ISAIAH 43:1–2 MSG

God sets the lonely in families,
he leads forth the prisoners with singing;
but the rebellious live in a sun-scorched land.

PSALM 68:6 NIV

PAIN

■ I'll never forget the trouble, the utter lostness,
   the taste of ashes, the poison
   I've swallowed.
I remember it all—oh, how well I remember—
   the feeling of hitting the bottom.
But there's one other thing I remember,
   and remembering, I keep a grip on hope:
God's loyal love couldn't have run out,
   his merciful love couldn't have dried up.

LAMENTATIONS 3:19–22 MSG

■ I learned God-worship when my pride
   was shattered.
Heart-shattered lives ready for love
   don't for a moment escape God's notice.

PSALM 51:17 MSG

Because God's children are human beings—made of flesh and blood—the Son also became flesh and blood. For only as a human being could he die, and only by dying could he break the power of the devil, who had the power of death. Only in this way could he set free all who have lived their lives as slaves to the fear of dying.

We also know that the Son did not come to help angels; he came to help the descendants of Abraham. Therefore, it was necessary for him to be made in every respect like us, his brothers and sisters, so that he could be our merciful and faithful High Priest before God. Then he could offer a sacrifice that would take away the sins of the people. Since he himself has gone through suffering and testing, he is able to help us when we are being tested.

HEBREWS 2:14–18 NLT

As a father has compassion on his children,
   so the LORD has compassion on those
   who fear him.

PSALM 103:13 NIV

Be merciful to me, LORD, for I am faint;
   O LORD, heal me, for my bones are in
   agony.

PSALM 6:2 NIV

Though he slay me, yet will I hope in him.

JOB 13:15 NIV

For he has not ignored or belittled the
   suffering of the needy.
He has not turned his back on them,
   but has listened to their cries for help.

PSALM 22:24 NLT

■ Pray that our LORD will make us strong
and give us peace.

PSALM 29:11 CEV

■ You've kept track of my every toss and turn
through the sleepless nights,
Each tear entered in your ledger,
each ache written in your book.

PSALM 56:8 MSG

REJECTION

■ But Zion said, "I don't get it. God has left me.
My Master has forgotten I even exist."
[And God replied,] "Can a mother forget the
   infant at her breast, walk away from the
   baby she bore?
But even if mothers forget,
   I'd never forget you—never.
Look, I've written your names on the backs
   of my hands.
The walls you're rebuilding are never out
   of my sight.
Your builders are faster than your wreckers.
The demolition crews are gone for good.
Look up, look around, look well!
See them all gathering, coming to you?
As sure as I am the living God."

ISAIAH 49:14–16 MSG

155

■ God assured us, "I'll never let you down,
never walk off and leave you."

HEBREWS 13:5 MSG

■ There are "friends" who destroy each other,
but a real friend sticks closer than a brother.

PROVERBS 18:24 NLT

REMORSE

■ Godly sorrow brings repentance that leads to salvation and leaves no regret, but worldly sorrow brings death.

2 CORINTHIANS 7:10 NIV

■ Be strong and take heart,
  all you who hope in the LORD.

PSALM 31:24 NIV

■ He personally carried our sins
  in his body on the cross
so that we can be dead to sin
  and live for what is right.
By his wounds you are healed.

1 PETER 2:24 NLT

■ In him we have redemption through his blood,
the forgiveness of sins, in accordance with the
riches of God's grace that he lavished on us
with all wisdom and understanding.

EPHESIANS 1:7–8 NIV

■ "Come now, let's settle this,"
    says the LORD.
"Though your sins are like scarlet,
    I will make them as white as snow.
Though they are red like crimson,
    I will make them as white as wool."

ISAIAH 1:18 NLT

SADNESS

■ Praise be to the God and Father of our Lord
Jesus Christ, the Father of compassion and
the God of all comfort.

2 CORINTHIANS 1:3 NIV

■ For you, O LORD,
    have delivered my soul from death,
    my eyes from tears,
    my feet from stumbling,

PSALM 116:8 NIV

■ But you, O Sovereign LORD,
    deal well with me for your name's sake;
    out of the goodness of your love,
    deliver me.
For I am poor and needy,
    and my heart is wounded within me.

PSALM 109:21–22 NIV

■ And now, God, do it again—
    bring rains to our drought-stricken lives
So those who planted their crops in despair
    will shout hurrahs at the harvest,
So those who went off with heavy hearts
    will come home laughing, with armloads
    of blessing.

PSALM 126:4–6 MSG

■ The Sovereign LORD will wipe away the tears
from all faces; he will remove the disgrace of
his people from all the earth. The LORD has
spoken.

ISAIAH 25:8 NIV

■ Bring joy to your servant, for to you, O Lord,
I lift up my soul.

PSALM 86:4 NIV

SHAME

■ "You're blessed when you feel you've lost what is most dear to you. Only then can you be embraced by the One most dear to you."

MATTHEW 5:4 MSG

■ On that day you will be glad, even if you have to go through many hard trials for a while. Your faith will be like gold that has been tested in a fire. And these trials will prove that your faith is worth much more than gold that can be destroyed. They will show that you will be given praise and honor and glory when Jesus Christ returns. You have never seen Jesus, and you don't see him now. But still you love him and have faith in him, and no words can tell how glad and happy you are to be saved. That's why you have faith.

1 PETER 1:6–9 CEV

"Do not be afraid; you will not suffer shame.
Do not fear disgrace; you will not be
   humiliated.
You will forget the shame of your youth
   and remember no more the reproach
   of your widowhood."

ISAIAH 54:4 NIV

I call as my heart grows faint;
   lead me to the rock that is higher than I.
For you have been my refuge,
   a strong tower against the foe.

PSALM 61:2–3 NIV

■ I have stuck unto thy testimonies: O LORD, put me not to shame.

PSALM 119:31 KJV

■ Yea, let none that wait on thee be ashamed: let them be ashamed which transgress without cause.

PSALM 25:3 KJV

ONE MOMENT
AT A TIME

KNOWING PAIN

- **Get support.** Pain is an emotion that shouldn't be held privately. Find a friend or a family member who can share your burden and help you through the difficult days. If you can't find the help you need or feel like you're in too deeply to get out, meet with a counselor who can help you work through what you're feeling.

- **Recognize the loss.** When you've experienced a loss, the swirl of complicating emotions can surprise you. Get on top of them again by recognizing what you're feeling. Write down each emotion and identify the different facets of this situation that make you feel so badly.

Don't be crippled. Times of grief are normal and expected, but once you've grieved appropriately it's important that you take steps to move on with the life God has given you.

CHAPTER 7

EMOTIONS OF FEAR

I know that most karaoke singing sounds bad. And believe me, I'm not so deaf as to think that my own is any better than anyone else's. But a few years ago when the karaoke craze was taking off, I forced myself to do it. It wasn't because I dreamt of being a rock star or fantasized about making my own music video; the truth is that crowds terrified me, and I've always been terribly self-conscious of my voice. I did it because I was tired of my fears conquering me. Though it seemed like a small thing at the time, it proved to be a turning point for me. It showed me that I don't have to be ruled by my fear, and it's given me the courage to step out of its grip.

■ Julie, age 47, Wisconsin ■

ANXIETY

■ Do not be anxious about anything, but in everything, by prayer and petition, with thanksgiving, present your requests to God. And the peace of God, which transcends all understanding, will guard your hearts and your minds in Christ Jesus.

PHILIPPIANS 4:6–7 NIV

■ God cares for you, so turn all your worries over to him.

1 PETER 5:7 CEV

■ Can all your worries add a single moment to your life? And if worry can't accomplish a little thing like that, what's the use of worrying over bigger things?

LUKE 12:25–26 NLT

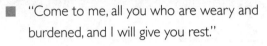

"Come to me, all you who are weary and
burdened, and I will give you rest."

MATTHEW 11:28 NIV

Let the LORD lead you and trust him to help.

PSALM 37:5 CEV

DENIAL

■ Should God then reward you on your terms,
    when you refuse to repent?
You must decide, not I;
    so tell me what you know.

JOB 34:33 NIV

■ Your Majesty, please be willing to do what I
say. Turn from your sins and start living right;
have mercy on those who are mistreated.
Then all will go well with you for a long
time.

DANIEL 4:27 CEV

■ Do not be hardhearted or tightfisted toward
your poor brother.

DEUTERONOMY 15:7 NIV

■ Don't be stubborn!
Don't rebel like those people who were
tested in the desert.

HEBREWS 3:8 CEV

■ Do not think of yourself more highly than
you ought, but rather think of yourself with
sober judgment, in accordance with the
measure of faith God has given you.

ROMANS 12:3 NIV

DISTRESS

◾ I was in terrible trouble when I called out to
you, but from your temple you heard me and
answered my prayer.

2 Samuel 22:7 cev

◾ I am in pain and distress;
may your salvation, O God, protect me.

Psalm 69:29 niv

◾ Consider my affliction and my trouble,
and forgive all my sins.

Psalm 25:18 esv

◾ I call on the Lord in my distress, and he
answers me.

Psalm 120:1 niv

■ Be kind to me, God—
   I'm in deep, deep trouble again.
I've cried my eyes out;
   I feel hollow inside.

PSALM 31:9 MSG

FEAR

■ Say to those with anxious heart,
"Take courage, fear not.
Behold, your God will come with vengeance;
The recompense of God will come,
But He will save you."

ISAIAH 35:4 NASB

■ There is no fear in love. But perfect love
drives out fear, because fear has to do with
punishment. The one who fears is not made
perfect in love.

1 JOHN 4:18 NIV

■ "My Spirit remains among you. Do not fear."

HAGGAI 2:5 NIV

But now, this is what the LORD says—
he who created you, O Jacob,
he who formed you, O Israel:
"Fear not, for I have redeemed you;
I have summoned you by name;
you are mine."

ISAIAH 43:1 NIV

INSECURITY

■ I praise you because I am fearfully
  and wonderfully made;
  your works are wonderful,
  I know that full well.

PSALM 139:14 NIV

■ Therefore, if anyone is in Christ, he is a new
  creation; the old has gone, the new has come!

2 CORINTHIANS 5:17 NIV

■ He gave his life to free us from every kind
  of sin, to cleanse us, and to make us his very
  own people, totally committed to doing good
  deeds.

TITUS 2:14 NLT

■ Before I shaped you in the womb,
   I knew all about you.
Before you saw the light of day,
   I had holy plans for you:
A prophet to the nations—
   that's what I had in mind for you.

JEREMIAH 1:5 MSG

■ The Spirit has given each of us a special way
of serving others.

1 CORINTHIANS 12:7 CEV

LAZINESS

■ If a man is lazy, the rafters sag;
   if his hands are idle, the house leaks.

ECCLESIASTES 10:18 NIV

■ Sloth makes you poor;
   diligence brings wealth.

PROVERBS 10:4 MSG

■ The lazy man does not roast his game,
   but the diligent man prizes his possessions.

PROVERBS 12:27 NIV

■ The sluggard buries his hand in the dish;
   it wears him out to bring it back to
   his mouth.

PROVERBS 26:15 ESV

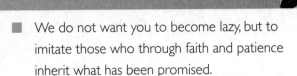

We do not want you to become lazy, but to imitate those who through faith and patience inherit what has been promised.

HEBREWS 6:12 NIV

All hard work brings a profit, but mere talk leads only to poverty.

PROVERBS 14:23 NIV

NERVOUSNESS

Trust in the LORD with all your heart
and lean not on your own understanding;
in all your ways acknowledge him,
and he will make your paths straight.

PROVERBS 3:5–6 NIV

Even strong young lions sometimes go hungry,
but those who trust in the LORD will lack
no good thing.

PSALM 34:10 NLT

The fear of human opinion disables;
trusting in God protects you from that.

PROVERBS 29:25 MSG

For God did not give us a spirit of timidity,
but a spirit of power, of love and of
self-discipline.

2 TIMOTHY 1:7 NIV

PANIC

■ "And if God cares so wonderfully for flowers
that are here today and thrown into the fire
tomorrow, he will certainly care for you. Why
do you have so little faith?"

LUKE 12:28 NLT

■ I, your God, have a firm grip on you
and I'm not letting go.
I'm telling you, "Don't panic.
I'm right here to help you."

ISAIAH 41:13 MSG

■ The angel of the LORD encamps
around those who fear him,
and delivers them.

PSALM 34:7 ESV

"I am with you and will watch over you wherever you go, and I will bring you back to this land. I will not leave you until I have done what I have promised you."

GENESIS 28:15 NIV

You, LORD, are the light that keeps me safe.
I am not afraid of anyone.
You protect me, and I have no fears.

PSALM 27:1 CEV

Only God can save me,
    and I calmly wait for him.
God alone is the mighty rock that keeps
    me safe and the fortress where
    I am secure.

PSALM 62:1–2 CEV

SHOCK

■ Pile your troubles on GOD's shoulders—
  He'll carry your load, he'll help you out.
He'll never let good people
  topple into ruin.

PSALM 55:22 MSG

■ God is our refuge and strength,
  an ever-present help in trouble.
Therefore we will not fear, though
  the earth give way and the mountains fall
  into the heart of the sea,
  though its waters roar and foam
  and the mountains quake with their surging.

PSALM 46:1–3 NIV

■ God is there, ready to help;
  I'm fearless no matter what.
Who or what can get to me?

HEBREWS 13:6 MSG

■ My flesh and my heart fail;
But God is the strength of my heart
and my portion forever.

PSALM 73:26 NKJV

■ Fear and trembling have beset me; horror
has overwhelmed me.... But I call to God,
and the LORD saves me.

PSALM 55:5, 16 NIV

■ The LORD is my shepherd, I shall not be
   in want.
He makes me lie down in green pastures,
   he leads me beside quiet waters,
   he restores my soul.
He guides me in paths of righteousness
   for his name's sake.

PSALM 23:1–3 NIV

ONE MOMENT
AT A TIME

OVERCOMING
FEAR

■ **Don't obsess.** Refuse to let fear rule over
you. If something is bothering you, either
meet it head-on or move on to something
else. Don't let fear paralyze you.

■ **Surround yourself with good friends.** Some
fears are good and will help you steer clear
of situations you should avoid. But some fears
are irrational, and good friends can give you a
loving push to conquer them.

Try something new. What would be a healthy fear for you to learn to overcome? Try something new that might be difficult for you. Are you afraid of being in front of a crowd? Find an occasion to give a short speech. Was there a falling out with an old friend? Find a way to reconnect and reconcile. Start with finding small ways to overcome some of the fears you may have.

Look for all the

What the Bible Says about…

books from Barbour Publishing

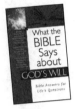

What the Bible Says about
GOD'S WILL
ISBN 978-1-60260-279-3

What the Bible Says about
WORSHIP
ISBN 978-1-60260-280-9

What the Bible Says about
PRAYING
ISBN 978-1-60260-282-3

192 pages / 3 ¾" × 6" / $4.97 each

Available wherever Christian books are sold.